DEDICATION

This book is dedicated to my only true father and helper of my destiny - the Most High God, Jesus Christ the Savior of my soul, who keeps me inspired daily with insights and direction.

Also to my dear and lovely wife Eunice Mayowa Tinuoye, and my children for their supports and dedication to the work of the ministry at large.

Finally, to all the members of house of hope (Christ for all Omega Ministry Worldwide)

FORWARD

The Prophetic way out to Uncovering your destiny is a remarkable book by my brother and my friend Apostles Segun E. Tinuoye. This book arrived at a time when it is most needed. His words of revelation and relevance stir my spirit and mind.

The truth and treasure in this wisdom is huge. Apostle Segun focuses his attention on the great importance in one discovering the purpose for which one was created which invariably points one to his/ her destiny. Discovering your destiny is so crucial to life because it's in discovering your destiny that you will find true fulfillment in life. The matter of destiny is a matter to be handled wisely.

For your life to produce result, you must understand destiny: maximum impact in life is a product of how much knowledge and understanding you have about your destiny.

Apostle Segun Tinuoye is one the wisest men I know and this book will give you extraordinary insights into the rearing of a generation that focuses on the most important matter there is which the matter of destiny.

No manufacturer produces something with the intension to fail. Every manufacturer has a manual that guides the user on how to effectively use their product and obtain the most from it. God is our manufacturer and He has a manual and the blue prints to how we out to function and achieve the most in live. Destiny is a path designed by God for you to follow in life in order to arrives that destination or pre-determined course of events.

The Prophetic way out to Uncovering your destiny is authored by one of the most progressive thinkers and communicators I know of in the spiritual sector as well as in the market place. His ability to stimulate and provoke contemplation on powerful insight that produces prophetic momentum with its resultant motivational force is unmatched amongst his contemporaries. Therefore, the book is a must read for all who desire to live a life that fulfills the original plan of the Almighty creator in their life.

Rev. J .O Ajayi

General overseer BFM, Former PFN Chairman Kaduna State

CHAPTER ONE

What Is Destiny All About?

CHAPTER ONE

WHAT IS DESTINY ALL ABOUT?

Jer.1 vs.5
"Before I formed you in the womb I knew you,
and before you were born I consecrated you;
I appointed you a prophet to the nations." **ESV**

What you don't define you cannot find. The issue of destiny is a serious one and should not be taken lightly. Scriptures says

Prov 16:20
Whoever gives heed to instruction prospers,
and blessed is he who trusts in the Lord. NIV

The matter of destiny is a matter to be handled wisely everyone in this life uses the word destiny in discussion one way or the other.

For your life to produce result, you must understand destiny: maximum impact in life is a product of how much knowledge and understanding you have about your destiny.

To actualize destiny, we must start with the definition of destiny, so that we can arrive at our destination.

Below are some definitions of destiny:-

- ❖ Destiny is the pre-determined course of events. It is the purpose or end appointed for a person or thing. All the occurrence of your life has already been put in place by divinity. Destiny simply means the happenings in the future of a person.
- ❖ Destiny is the experiences that someone has to experience in his/her life. A manifestation of divine plans and purpose of your life as predetermined by God.
- ❖ Destiny is the exact reason/purpose for which you

were created to fulfill. This is God's eternal plan and purpose for you even before the foundation of the earth. ***Ps. 139:13-16***.

13 For You formed my inward parts; You covered me in my mother's womb.
14 I will praise You, for I am fearfully and wonderfully made; Marvelous are Your works, And that my soul knows very well.
15 my frame was not hidden from You, When I was made in secret, And skillfully wrought in the lowest parts of the earth.
16 Your eyes saw my substance, being yet unformed. And in Your book they all were written, The days fashioned for me, When as yet there were none of them. NKJV

Before you were born God had a perfect plan and purpose for your life.

God's pre-ordained plan and purpose for your life is what we call destiny. Jeremiah :29:11

For I know the plans I have for you," declares the Lord, "plans to prosper you and not to harm you, plans to give you hope and a future. NIV

❖ God knows what He has planned for you. He has arranged and defined a glorious future for you. What is that future you hope for?
  Your destiny and destination in life has been written and predetermined by God and no man can change it. Isaiah 14 vs. 26-27

26 This is the plan determined for the whole world; this is the hand stretched out over all nations.
27 For the Lord Almighty have purposed, and who can thwart Him?
His hand is stretched out, and who can turn it back?

Many are in this world and passing through it without the slightest idea of the reason why they are here.

- ❖ Until you uncover your destiny, you cannot fulfill it.
- ❖ Destiny is a path designed by God for you to follow in life in order to arrive that destination.
  The truth is that you are meant to fulfill destiny. <u>You can only find what you have taken time to define.</u>
- ❖ Only the true meaning of destiny can lead to progressive and successful discoveries of ways to fulfilling ones destiny on earth.
  Beloved, as far as your destiny is concerned, the heaven has worked it out, it is left for you to uncover it and then fulfill it. It is a settled matter!
  God has purposed a very glorious and wonderful future for you. Don't live in ignorance because that is what the devil uses to hinder a lot of people.
  Ephesians 2:10
  For we are God's workmanship, created in Christ Jesus to do good works, which God prepared in advance for us to do. NIV

You have a destiny, one that only you can fulfill and complete. Your life is not an accident you have a great destiny. You are the only one hired or obliged to fulfill that destiny. Psalm 136 vs. 16

To Him who led His people through the desert, His love endures forever. NIV

Everything that will happen in your life is known to God Almighty. Nothing takes Him by surprise. He knows you. Common you have a great destiny.

God has given you a destiny. Something you are assigned to do in this life, something only you can do. It's in the uncovering of this something that brings out your fulfillment and greatness in life.

Before you were born, God has implanted in you certain visions, desires, ambition and drive to play a particular role in this history of your generation, you don't make history until you play the role, you are created to play in life. You are an actor sent to play in life. You are an actor sent to play a role in the drama of life. There are roles in life that only you can play. Your destiny is unique. There is no one in the entire universe that has what you have (personality, abilities, gifting, passions and experience) to do what, you are designed to and assigned to do in your generation. It is destiny that gives originality not a copy.

God has a destiny for you but He will not force it in you. God wants you to fulfill your destiny more than you do!

You need revelation to fulfill destiny. Revelation means to uncover.

Revelation 4 vs. 1

After this I looked, and there before me was a door standing open in heaven. And the voice I had first heard speaking to me like a trumpet said, "Come up here, and I will show you what must take place after this." NIV

Where you are born has nothing to do with actualizing your destiny. Jesus was born in Nazareth, a very little and remote village. This village was known for nothing good. But the savior of the whole world came from Nazareth.

John 1 vs. 46

"Nazareth! Can anything good come from there?" Nathanael asked. "Come and see," said Philip. NIV

The former president of Nigeria Jonathan Goodluck is from a remote village yet he became the President. It does not matter where you are born your destiny is what is important. Your place of birth should not put limitations on your destiny. Before you were born God had a perfect plan for your life.

Your parents don't determine your destiny.
Judges 11 vs. 1-40
***Jephthah the Gileadite was a mighty warrior. His father
was Gilead; his mother was a prostitute. 2 Gilead's wife
also bore him sons, and when they were grown up, they
drove Jephthah away. "You are not going to get any
inheritance in our family," they said, "because you are the
son of another woman." 3 So Jephthah fled from his
brothers and settled in the land of Tob, where a group of
adventurers gathered around him and followed him. 4
Some time later, when the Ammonites made war on Israel,
5 the elders of Gilead went to get Jephthah from the land of
Tob. 6 "Come," they said, "be our commander, so we can
fight the Ammonites." 7 Jephthah said to them, "Didn't
you hate me and drive me from my father's house? Why do
you come to me now, when you're in trouble?" 8 The
elders of Gilead said to him, "Nevertheless, we are turning
to you now; come with us to fight the Ammonites, and you
will be our head over all who live in Gilead." 9 Jephthah
answered, "Suppose you take me back to fight the
Ammonites and the Lord gives them to me — will I really be
your head?" 10 The elders of Gilead replied, "The Lord is
our witness; we will certainly do as you say." 11 So
Jephthah went with the elders of Gilead, and the people
made him head and commander over them. And he repeated***

all his words before the Lord in Mizpah. **12** *Then*
Jephthah sent messengers to the Ammonite king with the
question: "What do you have against us that you have
attacked our country?" **13** *The king of the Ammonites*
answered Jephthah's messengers, "When Israel came up
out of Egypt, they took away my land from the Arnon to the
Jabbok, all the way to the Jordan. Now give it back
peaceably." **14** *Jephthah sent back messengers to the*
Ammonite king, **15** *saying: "This is what Jephthah says:*
Israel did not take the land of Moab or the land of the
Ammonites. **16** *But when they came up out of Egypt,*
Israel went through the desert to the Red Sea and on to
Kadesh. **17** *Then Israel sent messengers to the king of*
Edom, saying, 'Give us permission to go through your
country,' but the king of Edom would not listen. They sent
also to the king of Moab, and he refused. So Israel stayed at
Kadesh. **18** *"Next they traveled through the desert, skirted*
the lands of Edom and Moab, passed along the eastern side
of the country of Moab, and camped on the other side of the
Arnon. They did not enter the territory of Moab, for the
Arnon was its border.

19 *"Then Israel sent messengers to Sihon king of the*
Amorites, who ruled in Heshbon, and said to him, 'Let us
pass through your country to our own place.' **20** *Sihon,*
however, did not trust Israel to pass through his territory.
He mustered all his men and encamped at Jahaz and fought
with Israel.

21 "Then the Lord, the God of Israel, gave Sihon and all
his men into Israel's hands, and they defeated them. Israel
took over all the land of the Amorites who lived in that
country, 22 capturing all of it from the Arnon to the
Jabbok and from the desert to the Jordan. 23 "Now since
the Lord, the God of Israel, has driven the Amorites out
before his people Israel, what right have you to take it over?
24 Will you not take what your god Chemosh gives you?
Likewise, whatever the Lord our God has given us, we will
possess. 25 Are you better than Balak son of Zippor, king
of Moab? Did he ever quarrel with Israel or fight with
them? 26 For three hundred years Israel occupied
Heshbon, Aroer, the surrounding settlements and all the
towns along the Arnon. Why didn't you retake them during
that time? 27 I have not wronged you, but you are doing
me wrong by waging war against me. Let the Lord, the
Judge, decide the dispute this day between the Israelites and
the Ammonites." 28 The king of Ammon, however, paid
no attention to the message Jephthah sent him. 29 Then
the Spirit of the Lord came upon Jephthah. He crossed
Gilead and Manasseh, passed through Mizpah of Gilead,
and from there he advanced against the Ammonites. 30
And Jephthah made a vow to the Lord: "If you give the
Ammonites into my hands, 31 whatever comes out of the
door of my house to meet me when I return in triumph from

the Ammonites will be the Lord's, and I will sacrifice it as a
burnt offering." 32 Then Jephthah went over to fight the
Ammonites, and the Lord gave them into his hands. 33 He
devastated twenty towns from Aroer to the vicinity of
Minnith, as far as Abel Keramim. Thus Israel subdued
Ammon. 34 When Jephthah returned to his home in
Mizpah, who should come out to meet him but his daughter,
dancing to the sound of tambourines! She was an only
child. Except for her he had neither son nor daughter. 35
When he saw her, he tore his clothes and cried, "Oh! My
daughter! You have made me miserable and wretched,
because I have made a vow to the Lord that I cannot break."
36 "My father," she replied, "you have given your word to
the Lord. Do to me just as you promised, now that the Lord
has avenged you of your enemies, the Ammonites. 37 But
grant me this one request," she said. "Give me two months
to roam the hills and weep with my friends, because I will
never marry." 38 "You may go," he said. And he let her go
for two months. She and the girls went into the hills and
wept because she would never marry. 39 After the two
months, she returned to her father and he did to her as he
had vowed. And she was a virgin.From this comes the
Israelite custom 40 that each year the young women of
Israel go out for four days to commemorate the daughter of
Jephthah the Gileadite. NIV

Your parents may not have planned you but you don't choose your parents. Japheth did not choose his parent but destiny has it that he will be a judge in Israel. Before your parents even met each other, God had a pre ordained plan for your life.

- ❖ Stop allowing age to hinder you from fulfilling your destiny. Many destinies have been frustrated or killed because of age consideration. If you consider your age, it is either you are too young or too old. You are destined to do great things in life. Jeremiah 1 vs. 6-7
6 "Ah, Sovereign Lord," I said, "I do not know how to speak; I am only a child." 7 But the Lord said to me, "Do not say, 'I am only a child.' You must go to everyone I send you to and say whatever I command you. 8 Do not be afraid of them, for I am with you and will rescue you," declares the Lord. NIV

- ❖ David killed Goliath if he had considered his age and refused to take steps destiny will be left unfulfilled. You are destined to excel in life.
Your ultimate destination has been pre determined by God and so the devil can't stop it.
Your destiny is the answer to the question; what has God called me to do in this life? It is destiny that actually gives you identity. You have no identity without your destiny. Ephesians 2 vs. 10
For we are God's workmanship, created in Christ Jesus to do good works, which God prepared in advance for us to do. NIV

God's destiny for your life will be consistent with the way He has wired or created you.
To uncover your destiny, there two questions to ask:
(a) ***What have you called me to do lord?***

(b) ***Who have you called and created me to be?***
This question points you to God's purpose and mission for your life here on earth. This is the ultimate win. God gets maximum glory, as you align with your purpose and mission here on earth; you get maximum joy and the kingdom of God is advanced!
Romans 8 vs. 29
For those God foreknew He also predestined to be conformed to the likeness of His Son, that He might be the firstborn among many brothers. NIV

Nothing separates like ***destiny***. You have a destiny and you have a destination.
Destiny is not a matter of chance, it is a matter of choice, it is not something to be waited for, and it is something to be achieved.

CHAPTER TWO

The Journey To Your Destiny

CHAPTER TWO
THE JOURNEY TO YOUR DESTINY

The moment you are born, the journey to destiny starts. The interesting thing is that, at that moment the devil our number one enemy will begin to do all he could to truncate that destiny.

Journey to destiny begins the very day one is born to this world, it is that very day that individual begins to have enemy.

Case study: Joseph, Moses and Jesus Christ

Joseph: His enemies who were against the fulfillment of his destiny were his brothers. "Behold the dreamer cometh, let us" they want to Truncate His Destiny but the End Result Was God's destiny for his life.

Moses: The first enemy of Moses was king pharaoh who tried to kill him and bury his destiny forever

But God had a great assignment for Moses, to lead the Israelites out of the land of bondage.

In like manner, God has assignment for you which you must carry out either the enemy like it or not. You will carry it out in Jesus name.

Jesus Christ, His number one enemy the very moment he was born was a king as well, **king Herod**. He pretended to be happy with his birth and God ordained assignment for him to deliver mankind from destruction.

But Herod was looking for a way to kill him and thwart his destiny forever, but behold he failed.

What do you think would have become of man if the king Herod has succeeded in killing Jesus Christ? It is better imagined than experienced. Yet God wouldn't have allowed that to happen.

Four basic principles about destiny

a. You cannot manufacture your destiny you can only discover or uncover it. It is already in God's plan and record, what He wants you to become. Travelling in the opposite direction like Jonah will only lead one to unfulfillment and destruction.

b. From the word of God, there are certain tools the Holy Spirit uses to uncover destiny to people. If you don't connect to these tools of the Holy Spirit, you will go to a herbalist to help you discover your destiny or even false prophet, and of course they will find one for you. There are three tools of the Holy Spirit to uncover destiny:

(i) ***Vision from God***: the revelation will just come somehow and you will catch it.

(ii) ***Dream like Joseph***: we know the story very well. You just have to be sensitive to your dreams. Pray for interpretation of dreams, the gift of discernment and discerning of spirits.

(iii) ***Prophecy***: (real one from above, not environmental prophecy). Isaiah 9 vs. 6-7.

6 For to us a child is born,
to us a son is given,
and the government will be on his shoulders.
And he will be called
Wonderful Counselor, Mighty God,
Everlasting Father, Prince of Peace.
7 ***Of the increase of his government and peace***
there will be no end.
He will reign on David's throne
and over his kingdom,
establishing and upholding it
with justice and righteousness

from that time on and forever.
The zeal of the Lord Almighty
will accomplish this. NIV

Isaiah gave the prophecy 600 years before Jesus Christ was born.

(c) God will not hide your destiny from you and expect you to fulfill it. The secret of the lord in with them that fear him.

(d) Once you can discover your destiny, it is in your own interest to know and to embrace the author of destiny. Habakkuk 2 vs. 1-4.

I will stand at my watch and station myself on the ramparts;
I will look to see what he will say to me, and what answer I am to give to this complaint.
2 Then the Lord replied:
"Write down the revelation and make it plain on tablets so that a herald may run with it.
3 For the revelation awaits an appointed time;
it speaks of the end And will not prove false. Though it linger, wait for it; it will certainly come and will not delay.
4 "See, he is puffed up;
His desires are not upright, but the righteous will live by his faith - NIV

Destiny is what will make you fulfill the original plan of the Almighty creator in your life. This is the reason why it's very essential to discover your destiny: these are ways; you could discover your destiny in the following means:

(i) Through prayerful enquiry from God
Ephesians 1 vs. 17-20,
17 I keep asking that the God of our Lord Jesus

*Christ, the glorious Father, may give you the Spirit of
wisdom and revelation, so that you may know him better. 18
I pray also that the eyes of your heart may be enlightened in
order that you may know the hope to which he has called
you, the riches of his glorious inheritance in the saints, 19
and his incomparably great power for us who believe. That
power is like the working of his mighty strength, 20 which
he exerted in Christ when he raised him from the dead and
seated him at his right hand in the heavenly realms,
NIV*

Matthew 7 vs. 7-9

*"Ask and it will be given to you; seek and you will find;
knock and the door will be opened to you. 8 For everyone
who asks receives; he who seeks finds; and to him who
knocks, the door will be opened.
9 "Which of you, if his son asks for bread, will give him a
stone?
NIV*

Psalm 27 vs. 4

*One thing I ask of the Lord, this is what I seek:
That I may dwell in the house of the Lord all the days of my life, to gaze upon the beauty of the Lord and to seek him in his temple.
NIV*

(ii) Through revelation by the Holy spirit

Acts 13 vs. 1-4

In the church at Antioch there were prophets and teachers: Barnabas, Simeon called Niger, Lucius of Cyrene, Manaen (who had been brought up with Herod the tetrarch) and

Saul. 2 While they were worshiping the Lord and fasting, the Holy Spirit said, "Set apart for me Barnabas and Saul for the work to which I have called them." 3 So after they had fasted and prayed, they placed their hands on them and sent them off.
4 The two of them, sent on their way by the Holy Spirit, went down to Seleucia and sailed from there to Cyprus. NIV

Romans 8 vs. 14
because those who are led by the Spirit of God are sons of God.
NIV

(iii) *Through personal revelation from angels.* ***Judges: 13 vs. 2-5***
A certain man of Zorah, named Manoah, from the clan of the Danites, had a wife who was sterile and remained childless. 3 The angel of the Lord appeared to her and said, "You are sterile and childless, but you are going to conceive and have a son. 4 Now see to it that you drink no wine or other fermented drink and that you do not eat anything unclean, 5 because you will conceive and give birth to a son. No razor may be used on his head, because the boy is to be a Nazirite, set apart to God from birth, and he will begin the deliverance of Israel from the hands of the Philistines." NIV

, Matthew 2 vs. 18-23.
"A voice is heard in Ramah, weeping and great mourning, Rachel weeping for her children and refusing to be comforted, because they are no more."
19 after Herod died, an angel of the Lord appeared in a dream to Joseph in Egypt 20 and said, "Get up, take the child and his mother and go to the land of Israel, for those

who were trying to take the child's life are dead."
21 So he got up, took the child and his mother and went to the land of Israel. 22 but when he heard that Archelaus was reigning in Judea in place of his father Herod, he was afraid to go there. Having been warned in a dream, he withdrew to the district of Galilee, 23 and he went and lived in a town called Nazareth. So was fulfilled what was said through the prophets: "He will be called a Nazarene." NIV

(iv) Through personal revelation and inward witness, Acts: 7 vs. 22-25.

Moses was educated in all the wisdom of the Egyptians and was powerful in speech and action.
23 "When Moses was forty years old, he decided to visit his fellow Israelites. 24 He saw one of them being mistreated by an Egyptian, so he went to his defense and avenged him by killing the Egyptian. 25 Moses thought that his own people would realize that God was using him to rescue them, but they did not NIV

(v) Through revelation in dreams from God, Gen. 37 vs. 5-20

Joseph had a dream, and when he told it to his brothers, they hated him all the more. 6 He said to them, "Listen to this dream I had: 7 We were binding sheaves of grain out in the field when suddenly my sheaf rose and stood upright, while your sheaves gathered around mine and bowed down to it."
8 His brothers said to him, "Do you intend to reign over us? Will you actually rule us?" And they hated him all the more because of his dream and what he had said. 9 Then he had another dream, and he told it to his brothers. "Listen," he said, "I had another

dream, and this time the sun and moon and eleven stars were bowing down to me."
10 When he told his father as well as his brothers, his father rebuked him and said, "What is this dream you had? Will your mother and I and your brothers actually come and bow down to the ground before you?" NIV,

Judges: 7 vs. 13-15
Gideon arrived just as a man was telling a friend his dream. "I had a dream," he was saying. "A round loaf of barley bread came tumbling into the Midianite camp. It struck the tent with such force that the tent overturned and collapsed."
14 His friend responded, "This can be nothing other than the sword of Gideon son of Joash, the Israelite. God has given the Midianites and the whole camp into his hands.
15 When Gideon heard the dream and its interpretation, he worshiped God. He returned to the camp of Israel and called out, "Get up! The Lord has given the Midianite camp into your hands." NIV

(vi) Through observation either personally or by others or trends, patterns, passions or interests. Luke 2 vs. 19
But Mary treasured up all these things and pondered them in her heart. NIV

Proverb 11 vs. 14
For lack of guidance a nation falls, but many advisers make victory sure. NIV
Proverbs 27 vs. 17
As iron sharpens iron, so one man sharpens another. NIV

CHAPTER THREE

Fulfilling Prophetic Destiny

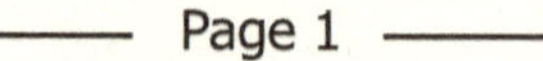

CHAPTER THREE
FULFILLING PROPHETIC DESTINY

Proverbs 23 vs. 18

There is surely a future hope for you, and your hope will not be cut off. NIV

To fulfill your prophetic destiny, you must be sure that your expectation shall not be cut short. Having discovered destiny, you have to pursue its fulfillment. You must know what it takes to fulfill your God-given destiny, nothing just happens!

The word fulfill has several meanings. It means: perfect, achievement, implementation, performance, satisfaction, attainments of goals.

You can remember Mary and what she said to the angel: "how shall this thing be?" the angel told her… "The Holy Ghost shall come upon thee, and the power of the highest shall overshadow thee…" Luke 1:34-36.

> ***"How will this be," Mary asked the angel, "since I am a virgin?"***
>
> ***35 The angel answered, "The Holy Spirit will come upon you, and the power of the Most High will overshadow you. So the holy one to be born will be called the Son of God.***
>
> ***36 Even Elizabeth your relative is going to have a child in her old age, and she who was said to be barren is in her sixth month. NIV***

There are certain things required of you to make your destiny a reality. In actualizing your destiny you must do things that make it a reality.

1. You must have true relationship with God: God is the giver of destiny. It is very important to have a true relationship with Him if you must fulfill your destiny. As

far as destiny is concerned only God can help you reach fulfillment. You must know Him as your savior and lord of your life. Have God in your life; deliver to you all you need to make your destiny a reality. Dan 11 vs. 32 ***With flattery he will corrupt those who have violated the covenant, but the people who know their God will firmly resist him. NIV***

When you know God well, the power to reach your destiny in released. To know only the true God is to be born again, acknowledge you are a sinner and repent, forsake all your sinful ways.

2. Your service to God: there is nothing that accelerates the fulfillment of destiny like service. Job 35 vs. 11 ***who teaches more to us than to the beasts of the earth and makes us wiser than the birds of the air?' NIV***
   Once you offer God, the best service you will stir God to make way for you to reach your destiny. Fulfilling destiny is possible through genuine service to God and His kingdom. Acts 10 vs. 35 who teaches more to us than to the beasts of the earth and makes us wiser than the birds of the air?' NIV
   Acts 10:35-36
   but accepts men from every nation who fear him and do what is right. NIV.
   As long as you serve God, you are accepted by Him no matter your nation nor tribe. True service is the access to the heart of God. Your place in the heart of God, is what make Him to work out your destiny.

True destiny-points why you are here! You must know your purpose/reason why you are here on earth. Only purposeful people fulfill their destiny. It is the pursuit of divine purpose that is the fulfillment of destiny. John 3 vs. 8b
The wind blows wherever it pleases. You hear its sound, but

you cannot tell where it comes from or where it is going. So it is with everyone born of the Spirit." NIV

3. Jesus' destiny was only fulfilled because He lived to pursue the purpose for which He came to the earth. The above scripture reveals that purpose for His manifestation here. Purpose makes you create time for assignment and so doing, you reach your destiny. When your purpose is known and defined you can now easily fulfill your destiny. Definite purpose for destined purpose.

4. Association: to go far, you don't travel alone. It is a complete truth that you cannot fulfill your destiny all alone. You need people to get you to reach fulfillment of destiny. The right association (true friends). The associations you keep either help you to become successful and fulfilled or become a failure. Proverbs 13 vs. 20
   He who walks with the wise grows wise, but a companion of fools suffers harm. NIV
   Your destiny travels in the direction of the people you associate with constantly. If you must fulfill your destiny then you must also keep away from some people.
5. Be hardworking: proverbs 10 vs. 4
   4 Lazy hands make a man poor, but diligent hands bring wealth. NIV

Proverbs 22 vs. 29

Do you see a man skilled in his work? He will serve before kings; he will not serve before obscure men. NIV

Proverbs 26 vs.13-15

The sluggard says, "There is a lion in the road, a fierce lion

roaming the streets!"
14 As a door turns on its hinges, so a sluggard turns on his bed.
15 The sluggard buries his hand in the dish; he is too lazy to bring it back to his mouth. NIV

A lazy man cannot fulfill destiny. Your work defines your destiny. See a man that is a hard worker, he gets to prominence in life. If hard work is the only way to get your destiny fulfillment then get ready to be a hard-worker. In every labor, there is profit. Handwork does not kill!

6. Be prayerful: things turn out excellently when we pray. You can only fulfill your destiny when you understand the power of prayer. To be prayerful is to be powerful and to be powerful is to be established. 1 chronicles 4:10 ***Jabez cried out to the God of Israel, "Oh, that you would bless me and enlarge my territory! Let your hand be with me, and keep me from harm so that I will be free from pain." And God granted his request. NIV***

   Once you prevail in the place of prayer, you will succeed in your life. Take time to pray about your destiny. The devil is out to see that your destiny is not fulfilled; you can stop him by praying and becoming more prayerful.

CHAPTER FOUR

Destiny Helpers

CHAPTER FOUR
DESTINY HELPERS

1 Chronicle 12 vs. 22
Day after day men came to help David, until he had a great army, like the army of God. NIV
We have defined destiny and the journey to destiny. You have a purpose to fulfill in this life which helps in the realization of your destiny. There are high places in life that heaven has programmed for your reach.
The divine plans and purpose of God has pre-ordained for you to actualize or accomplish cannot be achieved by you alone. God has arranged on ground men (people) to help you reach your destiny. These people will help you do something that makes the task of destiny become easy for you.

God has prepared certain people I call destiny helpers. Destiny helpers are under order/command to help you. They cannot refuse to help you because they are bound by Gods order to do so. Men were coming to David; day by day to help him. The journey to your destiny is faster when your helpers appear in good time.
The man at the pool of Bethesda stayed a long time in that condition all because he had no man to help him.
John 5 vs. 7
"Sir," the invalid replied, "I have no one to help me into the pool when the water is stirred. While I am trying to get in, someone else goes down ahead of me." NIV
The earlier you meet destiny helpers the better. Men under divine obligation to help you achieve what God has planned and programmed for your life.
These destiny helpers are those God has positioned and placed on your path to the actualization of your divine

destiny. They are on earth primarily to assist you in accomplishing your God given assignment on earth. You need to meet them at every point of your journey to the fulfillment of destiny.

Your life cannot be all that God has designed it to be without destiny helpers. These helpers have different kind of contributions to make in order to bring fruition to your destiny.

Let's see the various ways destiny helpers can get involved in your life.

1. Destiny helpers can be those that God has arranged on ground to teach and instruct you in your journey to realization of your purpose. They can be your mentors, pastors, prophet and teachers. Philippians 4 vs. ***9 whatever you have learned or received or heard from me, or seen in me - put it into practice. And the God of peace will be with you. NIV***

2. There are those destiny helpers who are assigned with assignment to give you finance and other things to make you achieve your destiny. Luke 8:3 ***joanna the wife of Cuza, the manager of Herod's household; Susanna; and many others. These women were helping to support them out of their own means. NIV***
   2 Kings 4 vs. 8-11,
   One day Elisha went to Shunem. And a well-to-do woman was there, who urged him to stay for a meal. So whenever he came by, he stopped there to eat. 9 She said to her husband, "I know that this man who often comes our way is a holy man of God. 10 Let's make a small room on the roof and put in it a bed and a table, a chair and a lamp for him. Then he can stay there whenever he comes to us."

11 One day when Elisha came, he went up to his room and lay down there. NIV

1Kings 17 vs. 2-4

Then the word of the Lord came to Elijah: 3 "Leave here, turn eastward and hide in the Kerith Ravine, east of the Jordan. 4 You will drink from the brook, and I have ordered the ravens to feed you there." NIV

I love verse a, "behold I have commanded a widow woman there to sustain thee (1Kings 17 vs. 9)

3. There is that destiny helper whose assignment is to connect and link you up with opportunities and people.

4. There are those, whose major assignment is to stand in the gap for you in prayer. They are those praying for you, until they see that your destiny is fulfilled.

5. There are those destiny helpers that are always there and ever-ready to assist you at any moment you need assistance.

6. Also there are those whose assignment is to serve and encourage you until your destiny is realized.

The sweetness of life is when your destiny helpers show up on time. The struggles most people are going through, ends the moment, their destiny helpers appear. Meaningful life is a life with help.

Your destiny helpers are heaven positioned booster of your destiny. You must do all you can to locate your destiny helpers.

1. Esther had a destiny to be a queen, but there was a modecai sent by God as her destiny helper. The truth is that without modecai, Esther would have ended up a nobody and without fulfilled destiny.

2. Jethro and Moses: Jethro was a destiny helper to Moses Ex 18. He went to meet Moses and advised him on how to appoint delicate elders to attend to the people. He gave Moses wise counsel. The little lad in Jesus crusade. John 6:5-12.
When Jesus looked up and saw a great crowd coming toward him, he said to Philip, "Where shall we buy bread for these people to eat?" 6 He asked this only to test him, for he already had in mind what he was going to do.
7 Philip answered him, "Eight months' wages would not buy enough bread for each one to have a bite!"
8 Another of his disciples, Andrew, Simon Peter's brother, spoke up,
9 "Here is a boy with five small barley loaves and two small fish, but how far will they go among so many?"
10 Jesus said, "Have the people sit down." There was plenty of grass in that place, and the men sat down, about five thousand of them.
11 Jesus then took the loaves, gave thanks, and distributed to those who were seated as much as they wanted. He did the same with the fish.
12 When they had all had enough to eat, he said to his disciples, "Gather the pieces that are left over. Let nothing be wasted." NIV

3. The last five loaves and two fish, fed the crowd, helped Jesus to feed the people as a destiny helper.

4. Joseph the butler and the baker: gen 40 vs. 6-
7 when Joseph came to them the next morning, he saw that they were dejected. 7 So he asked Pharaoh's officials who were in custody with him in his master's house, "Why are your faces so sad today?" NIV
Joseph helped the butler to reach his destiny.

5. Neman the captain of Syria was destined to recover from leprosy. The little maid was the link to the prophet. Without the little girl, great Neman would have ended up a leper for life. Elijah the widow of zarephath: 1kings 17 vs. 12/13
"As surely as the Lord your God lives," she replied, "I don't have any bread - only a handful of flour in a jar and a little oil in a jug. I am gathering a few sticks to take home and make a meal for myself and my son, that we may eat it - and die."
13 Elijah said to her, "Don't be afraid. Go home and do as you have said. But first make a small cake of bread for me from what you have and bring it to me, and then make something for yourself and your son. NIV

6. God saved the widows life from death and sent Elijah to help her.

LOCATING THESE DESTINY HELPERS

These destiny helpers are all around us but there is a need to connect and locate to them quickly.

Only God can connect you to your destiny helpers. Look up to Him and you will locate your helpers. Psalm 121 vs. 1-2.

I lift up my eyes to the hills - where does my help come from? 2 My help comes from the Lord, the Maker of heaven and earth. NIV

You will locate and attract destiny helpers through the help of

the Holy Spirit. John 16 vs. 13.
But when he, the Spirit of truth, comes, he will guide you into all truth. He will not speak on his own; he will speak only what he hears, and he will tell you what is yet to come. NIV

Your destiny helpers will find and locate you and help you fulfill your destiny. It is either you locate them or they locate you. Whichever way, God chooses to make you find destiny helpers.

Pray for God to connect you to destiny helpers. John 16 vs. 23
In that day you will no longer ask me anything. I tell you the truth, my Father will give you whatever you ask in my name. NIV

Be on your assignment and destiny helpers will find you. You must be where God's assignment for your life is then He will send you destiny helpers.

Destiny killers

Destiny killers are those who will not allow you to get to your destiny.

The four friends tried to get their paralyzed friends through the door but the people around Jesus listening to the sermon wouldn't allow them. They were not bothered about the condition of the paralyzed man; they didn't make way for them to see Jesus. They have no compassion; they diverted the friends from getting through Jesus. They are destiny killers.

Destiny killers block your dreams. They divert your destiny, they cause delay, they frustrate your efforts, and they only see the negative side of you, they are killers of Joy.

Destiny killers tells you your vision is too big, they drag you back and when they have dreams concerning you, such dreams are full of calamities.

Destiny killers are discouragement, they are wasters they waste your time and your life; they limit you and mock you. Some destiny killers are in your household, in church and around you. Destiny killers are bent on abolishing your destiny. Ecclesiastes 10 vs. 5-7.

> ***There is an evil I have seen under the sun, the sort of error that arises from a ruler:***
> ***6 Fools are put in many high positions, while the rich occupy the low ones.***
> ***7 I have seen slaves on horseback***

Destiny killers weaken your faith.

CHAPTER FIVE

Barriers To Destiny

CHAPTER FIVE
BARRIERS TO DESTINY

God has a purpose a mission, a calling and destiny for every person. You are not an accident. God planned your life before He sent you here on earth. Your parents may not have planned you. You have ultimate destiny in God. So make sure that you have a responsibility of aligning with Gods purpose and be ready to live out this plan for your life.
There are certain barriers that can derail the pursuit of your destiny

1. Spiritual barrier: Isaiah 1 vs. 18-20,
"Come now, let us reason together,"
says the Lord. "Though your sins are like scarlet, they shall be as white as snow; though they are red as crimson, they shall be like wool.
19 If you are willing and obedient, you will eat the best from the land;
20 but if you resist and rebel, you will be devoured by the sword." For the mouth of the Lord has spoken. NIV

Disobedience to divine instructions is one of the greatest barriers that can stand on this path of an individual who wants to fulfill destiny.

Divine instruction is the key to fulfilling your prophetic destiny, whatever makes you to walk in disobedience, wants to hinder you from enjoying the complete blessings. Don't walk away from God's word. Obedience is the secret to fulfilled destiny Job 36 vs. 11
If they obey and serve him, they will spend the rest of their days in prosperity and their years in contentment. NIV

2. Mental barrier: Proverbs 23 vs. 7
for he is the kind of man who is always thinking about the cost. "Eat and drink," he says to you, but his heart is not with you. NIV
Mentality sponsors destiny. How you think about yourself is very important to the fulfillment of your God given destiny.
Poor self- image can be a barrier to your destiny. Negative mindsets about yourself and your purpose is an enemy to your destiny
Examine your thinking pattern, if you must fulfill destiny to live right, you must begin to believe and think right.

3. Attitudinal barrier: Proverbs 21 vs.19
Better to live in a desert than with a quarrelsome and ill-tempered wife. NIV
Bad attitudes can affect your destiny. You can have an attitude problem and not give it attention and it affecting everything about you. Attitudes likes being contentious, aggressive, argue about everything, stubborn, always quarrelling, troublesome, hot tempered and unteachable. Your attitude will either attract or repel people and favor from you.

4. The accusation barrier: Haggai 2 vs. 23,
"'On that day,' declares the Lord Almighty,
'I will take you, my servant Zerubbabel son of Shealtiel,
' declares the Lord, 'and I will make you like my signet ring,
for I have chosen you,' declares the Lord Almighty." NIV

Gen 41 vs. 42,
Then Pharaoh took his signet ring from his finger and put it on Joseph's finger. He dressed him in robes

of fine linen and put a gold chain around his neck. NIV

Satan is the accuser of the brethren. He wants to use your mistakes to disgrace and make you powerless. Satan would like to keep you powerless because of skeletons in
your closets. But God would like to treat us like a signet ring on His right hand to accomplish His work backed by His power.

All you need to do is to cooperate with God. He will work with you to break through thin barriers to destiny fulfillment

5. The companion barrier: Gods purpose for each of us differs, so do not make
the mistake of comparing your destiny with another person.
God sees things differently than we do. Nothing brings Him more glory than when you accomplish His purpose for your life

6. The information barrier: Hosea 4 vs. 6
My people are destroyed from lack of knowledge. "Because you have rejected knowledge, I also reject You as my priests; because you have ignored the law Of your God, I also will ignore your children. NIV

You have to break through the information barrier if you must fulfill your destiny.
Information brings transformation and lack of information brings transformation. The journey of destiny has already been mapped out for you, so you need, get all information that can carry you through your place of destiny.

CHAPTER SIX

Prayer Points For Destiny Fulfillment

CHAPTER SIX
PRAYER POINTS FOR DESTINY FULFILLMENT

Jeremiah 29 vs. 11,
For I know the plans I have for you," declares the Lord, "plans to prosper you and not to harm you, plans to give you hope and a future. NIV

Psalms 138 vs. 8
The Lord will fulfill [his purpose] for me; your love, O Lord, endures forever — do not abandon the works of your hands. NIV

1. Any power that has tied down my destiny break loose from my life in Jesus name
2. Where ever the stars have been programmed to disturb my destiny oh God manifest your power.
3. My father, if I have been disconnected from my socket of destiny, reconnect me by fire.
4. Every witchcraft register barring my destiny catch fire in the name of Jesus
5. Every proclamation of the power of darkness against my destiny be destroyed in Jesus name.
6. It is written: the year that king uzziah died, Isaiah saw the lord. Isaiah 6 vs. 1
   In the year that King Uzziah died, I saw the Lord seated
   on a throne, high and exalted, and the train of his robe
   filled the temple. NIV
7. The power of king uzziah in my destiny die, in the name of Jesus
8. Every incantation and ritual working against my destiny, be disgraced, in the name of Jesus
9. I reject rearrangement of my destiny by household

wickedness, in the name of Jesus.

10. O lord, anytime I want to make mistake direct me right.
11. O lord, let my divine destiny appear and let perverted destiny disappear.
12. I refuse to live below my divine standard in Jesus name.
13. I paralyze every destiny killer in the name of Jesus
14. Every damage done to my destiny, be repaired now in Jesus name
15. O lord restore me to your original destiny for my life
16. O lord, lay your hands of fire upon me and transform my destiny.
17. No evil family river shall flow into my life in Jesus name
18. I render null and void the influence of destiny swallowers in the name of Jesus
19. Let the spirit of excellence come upon me, in Jesus name.
20. O lord, anoint my eyes, hands and legs to locate my divine destiny.
21. My destiny shall not die in Jesus name.

www.ingramcontent.com/pod-product-compliance
Lightning Source LLC
LaVergne TN
LVHW040931150826
845672LV00007B/2299

* 9 7 9 8 8 4 0 6 9 4 9 6 1 *